Marcus James has gifted us wi
the human heartbeat and ech
His finely crafted and evocati
and-now but always evokes tl
before. He conveys the mystery of the specinc and
qualities of objects, time and space and by extension,
re-enchants the reality of all of us. This is poetry that ripples
outwards and catches us emotionally and intellectually—its
depths are mysterious and its surface, sparkling with light.

—Victoria Field

This haunting poetry aims at finding the mythic moment
when human and world embrace and create each other, and
something else shines through. Reading the poems, forming
their words in our minds and mouths, we see and taste that
'something else,' and remember it in our souls and our bodies.
Fleetingly, it is intimately present once more.

These are love songs in the fullest sense of the word, full of
yearning, circumspect and sad, for the sensuous and spiritual
presence otherwise outlawed by tepid IT dreams and peddlers
of the phoney or the merely factual, who threaten to drain us
and the world of meaning and delight. They deserve to be
read as widely as possible.

—Simon Wilson

Defiantly out of fashion, these finely cadenced poems sing out
of our present darkness. A vital act of personal witnessing,
they express our current sense of alienation and yet at the
same time evoke the redemptive power of the numinous often
lying just below the surface.

—Peter Abbs

RAIN

Marcus James

Anima Poetry Press

First Published in 2019 by
Anima Poetry Press
Cissbury
Ashfield Road
Midhurst
West Sussex
GU29 9JS

www.animapoetry.uk

ISBN: 978-0-9935966-4-3

Contents

A little knowledge, a pebble from the shingle,
A drop from the oceans; who would have dreamed
this infinitely little too much?

ROBINSON JEFFERS

Thy tree has lost its blossoms, and the rind,
Chopp'd by the axe looks rough and little worth,
But the sap lasts, and still the seed we find
Sown deep.

BYRON

INVOCATION

Come vast wind, numinous rains sacred
to those who write their names in dust,
who listen for thunder, who seek portents of storms
in uneasy sleep. I would break for you,

I'd yield like a barley field, hands
deep in the moistening ground, spin
crazy into your darkness; I'd rend cloth,
stand bodily within you tossing rain

from blinded eyes, forgetting house and fields
and friends—fingers, palms and breath
releasing, untying, dissolving in rain,
flying apart into the storm. So

come, vast wind, numinous rains—sacred,
inviolable, longed for: thrice blessed,
by those who listen for thunder, who seek portents
of storms in uneasy sleep, come.

PART 1
Time and Place

SOLSTICE STONE

Even around formica tables,
float glass and steel
a bus in the rain enables
a ray from the deep field
to strike the solstice stone —

a memory, like fret-limbed
hawks glimpsed from the road,
brittle rust on the wind.

In Memoriam

Kerosene and steel above America,
the sun over Florida, the Eastern Range,
and some god of men sets
a hand on Merritt Island. Rage
of LOX and aluminum, rage of welded
gores and insulation, rage
into a fresh heaven of steel bells,
coils and liquid hydrogen,
impossible rage of machine melted
gantries in the chest. Combustion dies
in turquoise, explosive bolts,
the interstage, and solids fired
for ullage of cryogenics in lofted
tanks and helium spheres, and turbo-
pumps for men strapped and locked
into airframes, men hurled
into silence who passed
beyond dawn and evening of the world.

Apollo! Born in Florida, Texas
and White Sands, child of love
and war and navy boys, of star-
struck nazi dreamers drifting in and above
the innocent lounges of Huntsville: violins,
chamber music, kids and tough
musculature; these and the other things,
these and wives, sweat and shoulder straps,

these and schoolroom flags and American dreams,
these and the aluminum fists on the pads,
a type of greatness awaiting
anti-type in futurity, in parabolas
beyond orbital joyrides traced
onto the face of suns. They peer
into an un-conceived future, race
on to the day Americans' fears
deny America's sacred need
and war and welfare trump the frontier.

But we have other thoughts and other dreams:
Icarus boys still shade their eyes
against the sun (though none like these
old men, these ones who trod lightly
on the ground and drove Mustangs, hungered
for flight in cabins at 5psi).
With data, with virtual thunder
come Branson, Rutan, Musk, the songs
of free-market fundamentalists.
The Olympic gods are gone
and the gods of Canaveral, of flame
and steel gantries, our civic gods.
Only human intent remains,
producers of electric cars and composites,
insurance salesmen. No one's to blame
for the ruptured tank, and a Virgin ship

explodes above Mojave; a man
dies falling for a chance of bliss
over California—fields of shattered
fibre and epoxy fluttering apart;
and we wonder: have our battered
souls been buried here at last
or are we standing in-between
the old world and the stars?

WRITTEN IN DEJECTION
June 24th 2016

You could write a song of England
but raise your eyes
and find her gone;
or else you might pass onwards
through alleys and parks,
a murmur of patriots
of many colours and seasons
(gathering, intensifying, pouring through
the intimacies of London: doorways,
arches, gratings, the great conglomeration
of ghosts you have in you) yet still
come to a sudden end of it in your mind,
a space opening,
clarity,
and wonder what will unfold there,
or else what name you might chant
or what herbs you may burn
in your suburban garden or townhouse
to bring back the dead.

I won't pass judgment.
It's not for me to make things known
that haven't yet come to pass
and may never come to pass,
or to hold you to your dreams

or to set you free of them.
I'm unconcerned with anything but the wind
and the ground
pressing back my feet to me
and the breath—

The breath is of me and in me,
the sternum is a boat:
it leaves on the ebb,
it heaves and falls and I follow
in the sternsheets and am free.

LUNDY SONG

They're lost. They sit
and watch their contents spin
like rings of glass.
Outside the wind bursts hard
against the stones
and blinds the grass;
the windows groan
but the sun will rise
to show no traces
of our people or their past.

The unchained minds ascend,
they dislocate from cadavers,
their lifetime's spent denying the rain.
We fell six thousand years, they say
but will not fall again.

Hey ho! Here *we* are,
and there's the wind,
the lighthouse faces westwards;
the ebb still opens out into a song:
the idea of America
though America is gone.

WATERLOO

This is a time for falling—the leaves
to the ground and the sky into grey,
and you into damp suburbs, into streets
where nobody hears your laboured

breaths. You no longer know yourself.
You have slept and taken the Northern Line
to alight at Finchley and Camden, and the Central
to Bayswater. You commute together unsmiling

from Watford in the rattle of dirty cuttings
between the flats and from Haselmere
to Waterloo, named for a battle of muskets
and powder and marching men, "the rain

increased, the thunder and lightning approached
nearer, and with it came the enemy". But our
wars are distant and vacuum-formed—both
foreign and at once familiar. The ground

shakes unnaturally, and the mind is torn
and the torso cut, and warm blood spills
from a screaming baby's gut. Forlorn!
No worse than death by sword or sickle

I imagine. But though the end's the same
the quality has changed. I won't say one's better
and one's worse but these *are* changes—changes
earned and irreversible, and they've settled

now. Our querulous bards tell tales
of all that life projects onto the eye
and though there's a shining essence laid
in things like the sun, these skies

don't tell. I could write of a masked woman
who tramples broken skulls into the mud,
or essay words to open into wonder,
but I can't excuse the sorrow, or the blood.

Steel

They came past sightless
walls and tyres, by concrete stairs
and razor wire, this slight
woman and her child, to where
I saw them momentarily at rest,
delicate by a kerbside annealed
in their soft shining, self-possessed
amidst the tide of London steel.

Midhurst Common, 2017

What is it, then, between us?
WALT WHITMAN

I call on summer to loose my tongue!
There in the heart-cleft of the hills
a brittle hawk hangs rusting
in the returning rattle of the Brooklyn Ferry.
You come up here for a glimpse of things —
touch the earth with the back of a hand
and the world unfolds for you; but you are
lost in what is no longer a new century
rolling pagan thoughts in bags
too small to even sense it anymore.
The hawk hangs there, rusting; your eyes
and the pines a mirror to the wind,
mirror to emptiness — emptiness shining
to enfold the mechanics of your brain,
blue jeans and a plastic watch.
Your summer's brought by bulk carrier
and Brooklyn fades, tatters, the endless
ending of belonging, the demise of westwards.

WIND

If time is a river that pours through the piers
then the river's a stunsail bleached by the sun,

the hamlets and towns, great chunks of their walls
and guttering and gables, blow out beyond Bristol
and Lundy and Hartland, out to the wastes
where the memory of the cell of the memory lies—
a symphony flying apart into the wind
with the sonorous bells and the lightships
and tales of men,

while up from the South comes Tristan de Cunha,
the laughter of sepoys, Inaccessible Island
and Nightingale. Everything blows
to the whorl of America,
everything blows,
and Ravel sits slumped in Parisian cafés
listening to jazz.

PART 2

Image

... one in particular,
the ruin of the moon
in the shape of a troll.

THE PROSE EDDA

You are still wrecked among heathen dreams
YEATS

Noah's Dream

The Lord visits Noah in dreams.

Outside children tumble in the dust,
Shem and Japheth walk up from the field and
Norea beats clothes on the rocks by the river
and shapes clay with thin fingers,

but Noah sleeps.

The Lord slides in, whispering over the tiles,
drops fall from the mouth into the waiting ear.

Noah sighs and turns over. Reeds rattle
in the wind beyond the window.
A fly stalks the beard with tentative steps
and linen clings to the sweat of the skin.

The Lord whispers and whispers.
The words lie sweet on the back of the tongue,
they gag in the throat.

But Noah's eyes are open.

The Light of the Moon

"Silence has within itself an invocation of sound,
  the absence calls the thing into being,
  and the unseen interpenetrates with the seen",
  she said quietly to him and the stars shone down.

I see only a town spread out below an old tower
block with bad plumbing: the empty streets
will fill tomorrow with disillusioned feet
as ever. Your dreams are dead as a pressed flower.

"My feet are lively enough, and well-illusioned;
  why do you find such a lack in things?
  why not let *your* feet go wandering,
  and see where they lead by the light of the moon?"

That is not the one I remember—the moon
under which we danced and hunted and heard
songs and tales by the fires. My yearnings
have gone sour—sullied by landers and teflon boots.

"It seems those boots have made a deep mark—
  deeper in you than in the lunar soil;
  but it was only ever a reflection you saw:
  what lay behind things, not what they are."

Without the unsullied image I see only darkness
and false hopes; whichever way I turn
are plans and explanations—I've been burned
by too much light and now the cinders choke my heart.

"I think things are not as bad as that, or as brutish:
don't you see your phrases flowing lightly,
and your words enjambed across the line?
And mine run to the line's end, yet are still beautiful."

FLOOD

Rain comes
and land becomes ocean.
The sanctuaries of gods prostrate
under kelp encrusted copper keels
and a woman's cry turns to water.

Flesh curdles and falls from the bone
and propellers pass over.
Corpses severed by bronze blades drift apart
as the storm surge gurgitates
on the blank clicks and creaks of the sea.

Sea Child

...in each face
by the cracking sparks there was that obvious wound
made from loving the sea over their own country.
DEREK WALCOTT

He knew the ocean swell as a child
tumbling in dust—the westward flight
of gulls and wind-battered East Coast banks
and shoals, the crumbling waves and lank
curtains of rain. He saw a storm in his mother's
eyes, a mast on the horizon; and while the other
children chased around the huts he saw
a heaving prow—the galley of the Argonauts.

We might worry for this child, and for all
voyages of boys bound by thoughts
of water, bronze and memories, the echoes
warped by page and screen to settle
in forms more akin to hope than the actual
thing. Imagine Noah turned and grabbed
the wheel, followed grander dreams than mere
survival, left his dove behind him and steered
a course to where the sea pours off the ledge
at the world's end. What happens when the legend
of a fall is followed by another fall that *denies*
legend, as we have fallen now, and like
the last time none of this can be undone?

But say our child grows up enough
to strap on some form of sword and set out.
What then? What ship will put about
to carry him when even the finest crew's
displaced by nodes and satellites and a new
certainty of location, and the once recondite sea
itself seems evident in a way recently
unthinkable (though it may still come knocking
with a force that's real enough, and no knowledge
of wind or position is consolation when the ship
goes down and the lungs are rasping the water in).

But perhaps this water washes up a few tight boards
with which he builds himself what he calls
a 'bark' and makes a sail, setting out with a band
of brave and hopeful boys as companions.
What will he seek? And will he meet a fierce-minded
woman or witch to help him? And I wonder why
she's washed up here where it feels she's no longer
needed or comfortable, and what she wants,
and who put a cyclone in her eyes so we can't get
a clear view of her—just an impression of the depths
of a woman's rage that can put out the sun.
We may moralise but *she* was his lover
first and, in fairness, he betrays her—and so
watch out! Or perhaps our child does not grow
up to journey anywhere for she is his mother.
I don't know, and that is the way things run—
a great story meets the particular and either
ends or carries on changed into another

so fast we don't know what's happening. And this
is where I place my trust—in shimmering
things, and the fact that Medea wears a veil
in my mind behind which are many tales,
and many women and endings, and these hang
over the empty places we have made and are in fact
more real because life can't be pinned down
like a butterfly—we can pin much down
but not the world.

                I like this child. I love
his hope, and the selfishness and courage
that clings to his sense of being alone,
and his swift-winged boat which has its own
problems and dangers sure enough but flies
in the face of cynicism; and I would help and try
to be a father to him if I can, and offer a father's
wisdom—which is not much—and hope he lasts
the wreck to build, perhaps, a lesser boat,
but will journey on and one day come home.

A STORY

No one coughs and no eyes smart around the light
that shines on the drifting ark.

Tell us a story! the children say—*outside is so dark!*

So we sit and we talk and the stars are a birthday cake,
a gale off Fastnet folds up into a box.

Noah tossed the ball to Shem,
Shem passed to Japheth.
Ham caught it,
Shem caught it.
Norea grabs it,
she swallows it whole,
she laughs like an owl.
She knows the place
where the gunwales burn
and the sea bursts in.
She has seen.

(and a yacht anchors in the cleft of the Crowlins—
a kettle, a prayer, and two sparks across the blackness,
blinking)

I'll tell you a story!
Last night a man fell from the deck of a cruise ship.
He couldn't believe it, knowing he could never be so lonely,
knowing he could never be so afraid.

Then he believed it.
Never was a man so unlike the waters he imagined,
never was a man so alone,
or the sea so like the greyness on the edge of nausea.

"Did he cry?"
"Oh yes, he cried, he cried!"

In Whiphill Wood a spider unfolds legs like cracked glass
under the humus.

Wings

Our ship grows wings against the moon.

The boy grasps the wheel,
the ship becomes a raven:
feathers sprouting soft
between the fingers
cool wind over the knuckles and the wide horizon,
clinging on.

Our ship wheels against the stars.

I know this boy like I know my own skin:
I too am forever young;
I too am clinging, with trembling arms.

The Doubtful Image

Jim made a bitter angel dance
and formed a space of beauty
in the mind while in the world outside

great rusting flocks of birds flew
aimlessly hither and thither
and the leaves piled up in mounds

in the gardens and streets
near where he lived and
beside the streams and rivers

where mirror-lakes formed
in which he glimpsed his face
seeing the image of a man who wrote poems

but was far too subtle and great
to speak of the moon

ii.

There's a reservoir of doubtful images
we experience as tired and out-worn
or use ironically, but Emily grabs all
of them and smiles for she's a witch.

For her the sun is full of bold
and solary things and virtues—
the heliotrope stone and vervain
and hyacinths and saffron and gold;

and for her the moon is bright
with lunary cats whose eyes change
according to the time and phase,
and geese and shards of selenite.

She inhabits towers of broken
crown and tooth where spiral stairs
outline the course of her affairs
and stars are reminiscent of hope;

but now the river's backing up, sweeping
stench and blood into the water,
and heart and eye and thought
collide and spin, and the wall is breached.

iii.

We've lost all prior regard for qualities—qualities which
were still to some extent impressed even on the Kaiser's
canals or the Crystal Palace or the great guns of the
Dreadnought. A house is made with utter pragmatism
now—or less than that, for even pragmatism has some
sense of pride in it, while we're reduced to essential
practicality. The image is impure—at least no longer
pure as encountered in the world—but still I'm more
with Emily on this than Jim, seeing the moon in terms of
depth and receptivity rather than as a resource or target;
and that feels OK because it was never the thing
represented anyway, but the expression of a principle in
the mind—as is Emily. And though the loss catches in

the chest and perhaps all hearts are a bit broken now, they were maybe always broken in other ways, and there are other expressions of those principles—whether in a pool found in the woods or a city park, or a moth settled on a wall, or making love when it rains. And in honesty much of the moon remains, particularly in the mountains or at house parties on summer evenings and this moon is greater even than that of Aldrin or Schmitt, encompassing matter and mind *as lived* and not just a region of space; and anyway, some of our images could perhaps one day be technological, if *technos* were allowed to wake and breathe.

PART 3

Love

Socrates: We said, didn't we ... that there were two kinds of madness, the one caused by sickness of a human sort, the other coming about from a divinely caused reversal of our customary ways of behaving?

Phaedrus: Certainly

Socrates: And of the divine kind we distinguished four parts, belonging to four gods, taking the madness of the seer as Apollo's inspiration, that of the mystic rites as Dionysus', poetic madness for its part as the Muses', and the fourth as that belonging to Aphrodite and love.

Plato

In Odysseus' Dreams

She was a snake—a beautiful bitch
whose forked tongue and teeth
were lodged behind beautiful lips.

We talked in the garden under a tree
tossing an apple from hand to hand,
whenever she laughed it was murder to me,

knowing her plan, lost in the slits
of Circe's eyes,
her smile, and the squeal of pigs.

I almost fall, forgetting the root
and the sword and the oath to the gods
and all fine intentions. But an owl hoots

to the setting sun, and I see the child
in the crazy daughter, and the grief
even witches know at times,

and wrap her in my arms all thoughts
of earthly love forgotten, and hold
her there, and she is caught.

Hoopoe of Spring

It was always too much a part of her
to seek a mirror in a man's arms and smile,
a woman of grief and empty spaces,
pale hoopoe of spring.

A dorado drowned in the angel wind
a blazing spire between the eyes
too drunk for homeliness or time,
craved an earthing rod.

Where is your man of long standing
your verdigris god, your god
of Venus metal—straw headed
man of laboured words?

Lost voices whisper in her mind,
reflections picked from memories of queens
and commons set in bloody womb
bring forth her life.

The stars rush in towards her skin—
daughter of men your chandeliers
hang above vacant lots and tyres,
that light you bring.

Light filters into *our* obscurity
through sheets of horn and glass—

glittering copper feet and hands
glimmering pain and need;

only she whose raised arms
greet the dawn dies wondering,
the woman of grief and empty spaces,
pale hoopoe of spring.

SILVER AND FLOWERS

I would reach out and set you free if I was able
and bring you in with me to sit and laugh at a table
set with silver and flowers—but instead pull curtains
close against a Bradford night's rain, uncertain
in the presence of another's field and memories,
and impress an image on your face. You bend
and take your violin and play—play a rage
at the evening's news till hunger and lies fade
out; and I sigh, remembering that there's no land
where a man may reach to touch his wife's hand
gently as she turns away, or a child stops to look
inwards, or where some aching piece of song or book
of poems is made, that's not been contested by violent
men whose words match my words, and whose might
will only grasp the vision of a blade. I draw one now,
forged steel and beautiful as the wind, and howl
but have no answer, imagining bronze spears shaken
at the sun, a ritual shaking of metal, and gifts made
by the will of kings—images cast on a rough floor
and timber walls, the reek of smoke, violence of swords,
and ankle-biters squabbling in the dust. No silver,
no music or flowers, just gold rings, glittering.

ii.

There are herbs and skeins of geese and silver knives
beyond those walls, though in the shadows eyes

that face three ways and dogs straining at the leash
and darkness in the sense of reptile brains and creeping
things, suffocation and blood. The circle of the womb
requires a feebler twin to have its life consumed
to feed the other one, no nicety of speech
or scent will change the fact: she'd lay eggs beneath
some larva's skin to eat the screaming thing from inside
before a single shaft of the sun. I can't avert my eye
from it, the image rattles in the brain, a lipless grin
that's gaping wider than the mind can even think
of. And now my words are tumbling through her hands,
and she is in the room with shrike-like eyes and stands
with palms on hips and sable coat and grimaces, and asks
if there's some mother's son who'd care to pass
beyond the rusty grate where three roads meet
and go with her, and hope to return breathing.
And I have no answer. I wish to stay here with the rain
that backs onto the night beyond the windowpanes
and curtains, while the city lights its candle. I've longed
for permanance—striven to make a solid place from songs
and question marks, a mark of everything we've groped
towards that seemed real and true, and founded in hope.

iii.

These are the simple, violent things that weave the generations
and caught me in your house: the immanence of being in gated

wombs of scent and blood; the cradle song that flatters
the senses; the image of a country girl in tattered
skirts who sometimes worked the orchards pruning
apple trees and bit the sweetings there, whose
lips carry the scent into the estates and shoddy
government training centres and dead-end jobs
where there is no felicity to be found except in her warm
mouth; and the hands and subtle finger bones that hauled
us in, bound to all the other hands in endless chains,
which are sometimes beautiful but always there among the pain
or laughter at the start and ending of everything. We may have legs
to carry us but in the end we're swept off anyway and the blessing
of silver and flowers I wished for you is washed away in wintertime,
carried downstream on a tide of buff river-water.

iv.

We face each other, you and I, naked of angel
and demon things except for those we half recall
like memories of the movies: two humans on the edge
of things elusive and half-grasped that at rare
times burst in and almost break the banks but are usually
only vaguely sensed on the periphery. And I think of you,
and about love and your skin, and your human hurts,
and the scent of different parts of your body and of certain
chemical reactions binding us molecule to molecule, wondering
how it will be when this is prised apart—we who've wandered
through the shopping streets and cheap arcades and admired
the foliate ironwork in the roofs that somehow seems to inspire

and encompass the best in both of us and touch those parts
that seem saddest and most deep. There's a laughing
child in you whose hand I hold at times, and one in me
whose rhythms alternately exasperate and delight you. We
are a subtle dyad, having memory of times when the river
was eternal and the streams and orchards inhabited—a wistful
hope on winter nights when the only magic was television.
I reach towards that child again with hands held
out and touch fingers. But I shouldn't speak
this way: our lives are a flood, a thunderstorm, even
the least of us explosions into being and light—though
we feel most the ends of things, forgetting we also grow
young as they pass till we fall on the ebb, washed out
among wading birds and the estuary mud and the sound
of cormorants, to change in the smell of a salt breeze
to amphibian, then fish, and so at last reach the sea.

Bloom and Flood

The flowers are in their bloom and flood and she is beautiful
among them—her arms, her blood.

Spells of grasping intellect can cast no bind on roots
deep enough to weather and to last—

she is beautiful, a woman of fifty years en-wombed
in flowers, she mocks the rifts

I find—fragments, plastic and metal—a harsher tomb
than that in which she's set

as queen. But a ladder leans against the tree for wind-bruised
pickings—the sweet blowing of everything.

Part 4
Shards of Glass

Shards of Glass

... faiths and empires gleam
Like wrecks of a dissolving dream.
Shelley

Say a word is a knife with the world laid
shivering and raw on the blade;
but hold the knife and call it a bird
and she'll grasp the world with delicate feet
and sing of the people and dusty streets
and the places their love was interred.

How would we seem through the eyes
of the dead? What say we don a tricorn
hat and look to windward wondering
on what's been lost and what found?
What of prophets in industrial towns,
or baggage handlers, or men pondering

rhymes on storm-bound submarines
in wartime?—dog-eared reams
of metrical verse for the ship's rag
off the Hohenhorn. What of disregarded
gods? Or the half-true words imparted
by some Mediterranean oracle?

Call these lines a hayrake table
merging old and new: a brave
resolvedness of form, chip-carved bands

to grace the edge and boards cut
first by table saw but
bearing the deft marks of the hand.

Say we put cynicism aside
and discard the knowing smiles
made only to glance round seeking
affirmation—discard them as a boatman
casts off the bow line—and invoke
some muse. So speak,

woman of innumerable days,
of the greatest things within you laid
in the breathing bones, and of the least,
and the canticle between them—words
forged in silver with a burred
hammer, let them fall around my feet.

ii.

It begins where the sun dips to the water
or behind a hill and livestock are bought
and sold; where time and weather coalesce
and the radio's slight static still sometimes
suggests the Home Service or wartime
among faint echoes of Taliesin.

As long as the sun sets in the eye
of the West we will praise Urien:
even in Dyfed where Strata Florida
broods in a subdued land

and choir and nave is spanned
on winter nights with an intricate vault

of stars by the Teifi. The hours
of freedom are dearly made. Power
passes to and fro, or lingers
over the ages' count of blood-
feud and bond and there is no justice.
I tap the warning out with fingers

that have taught the contrapuntal lines
of Bach in piano classes and ply
a delicate figure over the bass;
the hands that formed extensions
of themselves with plane and wrench,
and have touched the strained faces

of invalid relations. We travelled
home past a rainbow trammelled
on the hills and that farmers' pub
with the independence flyer stuck up
by pool table and hand pumps;
and by groups of kids, the grandsons

of presbyterian fishermen playing
in towns where not one boat remains.
In dreams we sit in homes of ancient stone
and listen to rain and wind beating
in across the fields, and braying sheep,
and doze beside the Abergwesyn road.

iii.

Beyond that road of dreams
lie city streets and cars: the neat
workplaces, trains and parks
of home-bound Londoners appear
in place of Rheged's men whose spears
and feats of arms have left no mark.

We enter the data stream. Urien
and the intricate lines of Bach are pried
from the hands and shatter into glass fragments.
I grasp a piece—reflections, memories,
the news and the eye's stark reverie
mark where ancient worlds are spent,

breath-dead. The incommunicable
fades in pursuit of the seemingly new—
blended light and shade, unforgiving
eyes and thoughts like corridors of dust.
But then I recall your voice and love
shows a way to return to the living

where the pattern set on town and water's
being fulfilled, the resonance born
on antique streets as much from pumps
and blocks and the quenching of steel
as the arterial pulse, and the sensitive
hand, and the river lingering in the blood.

You spoke to me, "son of man"
you said and I still repeat, a man
of memory, of the hand's knowing,
of your shoulders in the delicate hours
of your art, of your vertebrae, your power
clasped above and below, the flow

of our many lives and liquid
wanderings — strangers mixed
in tangled arms and looks.
But even such things as these are splayed
under the turning moods of the ages —
our flowers, pressed in an empty book.

iv.

Whose ownership, whose sense of right
wracks the glowering days' delight
in liquid words? And what black dog
mutters in the night? A tattered
coat tugs the ribcage, batters
in the gusts among the cars and joggers

passing in the rain. A great Shard
shades St Thomas church and marks
the moment doubt was smoothed away —
a certainty, a finger held to warn
against sentiment. But certainty is torn
from motion, always sure but never remaining

in one form; the endless abstractions
of thought, theorists and bureaucrats
littering cities like skins sloughed
in disregarded chambers of the mind.
Logic, reason, sanity, science?
fossils, handbills and puffs

of smoke! Men and women walk
and clouds condense and seagulls sport
far below the pinnacles of these towers
and float glass windows. And above
us the heavens charged with the love
images of pagans circle round

(though the image is of birds, the fleet
touch of wing-tips against the cheek
that bring a subtlety or shift, the momentary
alignment of knowing). Everything changes
in a moment *they* can never see, create,
or recognise, in spite of tarmac roads

and cryogenic steel, and all the permutations
of numbers. And all the while the blazing
worlds spin round and memory mixes lies
and truth like an oracle: our buildings sit
on bomb craters and patriotism and the spit
of farriers, and machines fill the skies.

v.

Night falls into fever under a rampaging
moon, the sweat and flame faced
revellers wandering in the booze
of small-town gardens, the candle-
dark of neighbours, gossip, and tanned
arms: these and the rampaging moon.

Whom do we carouse with round the fires
or laid aback with tips of spine
or shoulder pressed to earth and grass?
We talk, but only for a glimpse of constellations
through the trees above the crenellated
roofs of terraces, overmastered

by the unexpected brush of fingers
on the arm among the chimineas
and paper lamps, assailed
by sultry wives whose thighs
and sweat encompass the desire
for love. Ancestors drunk on ale

and sack and pale wisps of laughter
pass among the tentative handfastings
and tongues: their thoughtless copulations
our demise, our fall in each moment,
their passage set in cartilage and bone,
the deep memory, redolent of nations.

We are the walking chattels of time
who project a winged image for a while
onto the screens of quaint picture house
or multiplex and are then discarded,
worn out from bondage to a half-
imagined life; ours the towns

where dawn comes as death,
as stale beer on the grass left
with last night's glasses and dreams,
half-eaten paper plates enough
for suburbia. But tonight nothing's
real in the sense our lives are said to be.

vi.

There's Hertfordshire, and urban train
lines in Birmingham, and the Yorkshire Dales,
and then there's Lowestoft with the bridge
and the Sea Lake lodged under the Urals
and the wind. This one's of curtains
of lank rain and sandbars, of flotage

and the memory of mooring buoys
and slipways: the old guys could haul
a smack or drifter up on the ebb
and change a plank with it all caulked
up before the tide. One time I walked
to town from the new marina, set

a brush of varnish down by the hull
of a motorboat, went mulling
these things so unaware I knocked
over a scavvy laying baseplates
by the road. You know how *they*
can be, but this one smiled lopsidedly

and told me he once worked on trawlers
"there's no money in it anymore"
and his father's father built timber
yawls down by the beach at Southwold.
But boats are made of fibreglass now,
shipped out to nose around river

estuaries and bars where they somehow
don't belong, like the yachts whose bows
shade the Victorian swing-bridge set
by the Yarmouth road. That night
the fenders heaved against the piles
and faint echoes of an East Coast swell

rolled up from Ipswich bringing dreams
of estuary buoys and lobster creels,
and lightships on the sands with vacant
galleries, their living-quarters all stripped
out and abandoned except when a Trinity
boat comes calling now and again.

vii.

We know the boat shed of memory
long before knowing the boat shed
of life—we're born with it set
in the brain. I stand
there surrounded by lofted plans
for yachts and mallet blows, and the bell

notes of vigorous hammers. But rotten
fibreglass and the crisp-packet flotsam
of the Sea Lake surround *life's* shed.
Inside we find the mind's
confusion: adze and angle-grinder,
copper roves among engine beds

and carbide tooling: toys for the rich.
Even craft is just a toy to the rich.
Iroko replaces exhausted teak;
whole forests lie between my hands
and rest in laminated bands
in the frames beneath my feet

among the white marinas—
here among the little heritage
ships whose binnacles and seams
and tales of men oppress our shoals
with a trace of torpedo boats
off Friesland and fire at sea.

Fear fire and water! An oily
rag left in a can may burn and foil
a lifetime's good intent if there is
or ever were so bold a thing,
and a man may drown in an inch
of rain. But in the harbour sits

the odd ketch or dory all roved
up from history's planks—an armload
of tight boards salvaged from lost
wrecks and Waveney silt and the dark
mud of the Thames: our hopeless barques
of hope and the water, gently rocking.

viii.

Fortune comes and fortune goes;
it comes to those who wait, they say, though
you may wait a lifetime and find
none. We moored where sun and stars
made lofty circuits of the hearth
and the cat sat singing my rhymes

among walls whose muddled history
settled into corners and crevices
like rust. One time we lit sage
and drove the spirits from the beams
with spoons and saucepans, dreamed
them into a night full of the names

of gods and constellations—astrologies
of power but uncertain provenance.
Then holding hands we left
the fire to cats and solitude and sloped
together through the dark oak
fretwork of the lanes and trespassed

on the Abergwesyn road where hills
sip from a porrón of stars spilled
from fords and wind-bent hawthorns.
Are stars in the mind less real?
We leant against a gate where field-walls
met the road, old stones brought

in memory of other mens' potent
hours—she with her tangled hopes
and muttered desires and I,
with a headful of schemes and hands
shaped by the age and circumstance
and an indolent nature. All of us lie

ourselves to sleep, but lies lived
well come true in time. By the bridge
the Brennig whispered in the dark;
there are things only science makes
possible: I ignore them here in case
my reverie is closer to the mark.

ix.

But still I wonder what it would take
to save the stars from vacuous space,
from sums and orbital telescopes
and propaganda. Mere scale!
The mind is not apart from the tales
it tells or the world it dreams on; hope

dies when it's said that to write of stars
without irony or from the heart
is sentimental. "My love!" (meaning
humanity: all those who've gazed
up wondering at the constellations
or made furrows with their feet)

"they're just old light" we're told;
the Plough and the Pleiades lie cold
in the lists of the dead. I draw a pitcher
of Lethe's water and drink deep;
I roll the stone away and peer
into the empty sepulchre; I sit

and weep over stars, can't sleep
for thinking of the sky. Either
galaxies are incidental light
or they clothe emissaries. Or both,
perhaps, and there lies our hope,
though with banded wings. I left

Bradford on a slam-door train
and ran up river as late
summer sun lit up the Shipley
mills like returning memories;
and by a road in Dentdale
found a limestone trough filled

with reamy water from a pipe
off the fells gathered like bright
cylinder glass—molecules aglow
with qualities as strange to matter
as the child's city is to the man—
things forgotten but always known.

x.

We make a centre where we stand!
and there the sun and planets
round the earth in monumental circles;
we make a centre where we stand
and comets burn their prophecies, and
Venus traces heart-shaped whorls

around the brain. But in Bedfordshire,
whose downs and bracken lanes led
on to Dunstable and Luton with its many yards
and patios, the barbecues and lawns
encased our mysteries and all
we did was turned to shards of glass.

The mirror breaks and every fragment
multiplies and spins to makes a thousand
glittering forms where there was one!
The mirror breaks to make chrome
facets, windows opening
onto piecemeal worlds, and the sun

tells no tales beyond the hours
and the inprescient moon goes sour
like abandoned milk. But all
returns to its original form impelled
by higher form; the world is held
in thought—carborundum caught

in a glass matrix like a grinding wheel,
a balanced disk that shapes or kills
with a moments inattention, spun
on whisper-smooth bearings. Listen!
vitreous fragments can coalesce
into ferns and ponds set under

woodland branches—scrying pools
for the subtle waning of the moon
where a silent woman or a man
may catch a glimpse of things when
wind patterns the surface or sends
gusts that blow back grains of sand.

xi.

All of this and more was told
in the Book of our ancestors—hold
a question, point and you'll find
your answer. But few seem to open
them now—they contain no hope,
even of divination. Bindings

of goat and pigskin fray and tatter
in bottom drawers, "I am that
I am", a seldom consulted oracle
of mildewed pages, an absent text.
But copies are still sent for repair
or to be rebound—family bibles

kept only for names written in pen
on the endpapers or out of a pent
up longing for continuity (though
everything changes, nothing stays
the same!—even gods are reclaimed,
harvested and gathered up for sowing

in fields or poly-tunnels, even Yahweh
and his only son). The God of our fathers
went west on gull-winged ships
but returned on the White Star Line
with rumour of Christian Science
and the Mormons of Salt Lake City.

Shall I tell you how empires die?
I know as much as anyone — I
was in at the kill in Cambridge,
and the better bits of London
in the late seventies where one
could still almost keep the faith

if one had the money. There was tea
at Claridges and cake, and appreciation
for order and good manners;
and women and war heroes blustering
about change and how the lustre's
gone, and the pain of no longer mattering.

xii.

They left a listless monument,
their sense of not quite belonging,
of being lost among the rocks
of Albion and the coastline
and borders of this and most
other places loved and pocketed

as a child — the loss of classroom
atlases and tall tales that pass
lightly over the truth and realities
of comfort and fine houses denying
what doesn't fit with the familiar lies
of friends. We moan and tally

up the least of things. But anchors
drag in every storm, and there are
hurricanes and worse off Africa,
and at Algiers people leave port
on boats some swindler calls
good enough for a passage

of the dispossessed, swindling lives
while I sit in Sussex writing
lines worth less than candles.
But still I write— and I expect you also
do *your* thing, meeting at the Fishbourne
hall each week, perhaps, for hands

of bridge or scaling some sea-cliff
on the West Coast; or those meetings
on the beach at Southwold with tinfoil
barbecues and fishing. One time
a barquentine ghosted the horizon
for hours as we lay there—spindrift

of history. Enough of such losses!
I take your hands, your soft
feet interpenetrate with mine.
Whatever path you've trod I honour
that of God within you, "on
with the dance, let joy be unconfined".

Epilogue

THE RUINS OF TIME

The mansion falls among the ruins of time, shuttered up,
though the yard still sees a few blooms turn their heads
among the shards and dereliction and a single window
open to the wind, through which I scramble, wandering
round the peeling rooms among the cans and butt ends of
a few kids who come in sometimes—and not only to take
photographs. And as I write, old Grandpa three doors up
comes shambling home; the lights are on and the kids are
grown but *their* kids still welcome stragglers, misanthropes
and any pedlars passing in the road. Fear fire and water!
Guard the house you made, for there's still a thing inside
turns over when breath touches the dawn.

So do not bow to my visions of despair, or the illusions of
crowds, or the genius in his attic room with his raging eyes
and moon:

so long as the diaphragm
so long as the heart
so long as the conflated thought and splayed fingers
so long as the balanced repose of the head
and the vertebrate spine
and the tongue on the roof of the mouth
and the breath,

for though the water and lands are all displaced
and all familiar form is washed away
we'll take our love into the grave.

Lightning Source UK Ltd.
Milton Keynes UK
UKHW010606240719
346727UK00001B/25/P